THE AFTERLIFE CONNECTION

THE AFTERLIFE CONNECTION

· SOFT POETRY AND COMFORT ·

A. G. CAPUTO

Crystal Place Inc.
PO Box 215
Cogan Station, PA 17728-0215

Library of Congress Cataloging-in-Publication Data 88-92650

ISBN 0-929484-00-2

I dedicate this book to my wife, Emilia
She is my friend and my love.

CONTENTS

We leave our bodies to wither away
Christ shines bright on this glorious day
We lift in love to an Omega direction
For who we were, we are a better reflection

An Omega direction? That step from life
Our journey forever, after life

My sincerest thanks to Cassell Ltd., London, England for allowing me the pleasure of redesigning some of their original artists' works.

For meditative depth of thought
May your heart feel the joy in these pages

THE AFTERLIFE CONNECTION

"PEACE IS THE PRINCE"

To understand love, we must feel life's pain,
Seems the heartaches must go on,
Then we all release to a pleasuring cease,
We are born to reach a new dawn.

We step away gently, to float with the wind,
For the wind whispers joy in The Son,
The Son is warmth, The Son is peace,
Peace is The Prince, is The Son.

Christ, The Son, gives life anew,
That our eyes aren't designed to see,
We must see with our heart to get a new start,
Then we'll know truest meaning of free.

Friend, lay down your tears with any fears,
For there is no death to be seen,
There is life forever, after life,
We go in peace with God to our dream.

"ASK"

Heaven bound, in silence or sound,
Joyfully with The Son,
The Son forever is Jesus Christ,
Our Brother is The Holiest One.

Knock on His door, it will be opened,
Ask and you shall receive,
In life and death, all He wants,
Is in peace, for us to believe.

"A NEW HORIZON"

As one must leave, one must stay,
It's only change, not death;
It's a new horizon under God,
His fragrance is our breath.

Life is for learning till we pass on,
It's called our earthly fling;
When the carousel stops, just step off,
Take a step to freedom and sing.

Sing with no fear, the other side,
For always The Son shines bright;
Son? The Son, The Prince of Peace,
Guides us with His light.

"THE PLACE OF AN INJURED DOVE"

A rainbow's not gone, it's just set aside,
In mourning we open our eyes,
But we go on to face a new dawn,
And ourselves become wiser then wise.

Death has no Alpha or Omega by far,
It is what we are born to be,
But along the way we must share and say,
I'll give my all, my me.

We must reach and share our beautiful life,
By touching another's star,
Then we will be of inner peace,
And the why and what we are.

If a lonely day does sadden your room,
Take the place of an injured dove,
Feel its hurt and pain, then yourself regain,
Be glorious and share all love.

"NOTHING EVER DIES"

For life and all its beauty from one day to the next,
We suffer long, and in silence,
Emptyness and lonliness run together going nowhere.

Smile in your heart as you keep pure thought,
Be the person you are, shed and share your dreams,
Keep searching for the rainbows.

For life and all its beauty from one day to the next,
We are loved in the stars existence,
Go forward and beyond yourself to be lifted in spirit.

Keep reality in touch with your heart as you become anew,
The splendor of life and friends can support you,
Positive awareness is easy.

Let your heart flow soft, gentle and wise,
Be everlasting goodness, nothing ever dies.

Remember our Brother's promise.

"THE GOLDEN ROSE"

In a field of daisies,
Be a golden rose,
Let your roots touch those who care,
Life passes by,
So very quickly,
Bloom, then die, but share.

Then bloom again!

"PARADISE"

As I step outside
From the inside of myself
I look back.
It seems like yesterday I was a child
Or, is it yesterday I was old, I am now as a child?

I am leaving the years, and pain in my body
The years and pain
They seem unimportant for they brought me to pleasure
This pleasure of my new beginning
We are created to reach this beginning!

I now touch that paradise I was born to see,
But I'll always share love with you,
My body grew older and older,
But my soul stayed young as I grew.

Look in your heart
With a thought we are together
There is no death

"THE AFTERLIFE CONNECTION"

Gently we step away from us,
Please lay your fears aside,
There's no more pain, as we regain
Ourselves in pureness and pride.

No reason to return, our future is there,
Where beauty is called resurrection,
At rest are we surrounded in love
From our bodies to The Afterlife
Connection.

Afterlife Connection? Purest affection,
Christ will lift our heart,
He makes us anew, me and you,
Death is our new start.

God touches our bodies to sleep.

"ONLY SO MANY BREATHS"

Each of us are allowed
Only so many breaths,
When life is done, it's
done.

Each of us are allowed
Only so many breaths,
Share with The Holiest
Son.

The purpose of each breath
Is to live in eternal love.

"OUR HOLIEST BROTHER"

Tears when we're born, tears with good-by,
Pains of life can make one cry,

Pains of death will make tears too,
Remember, remember, we are not
through,

Afterlife is where we'll be,
Our Holiest Brother holds that key,

Christ, it's Christ, The Chosen One,
Love from God through His True Son.

"A LOOK"

At the end of life's song is a new beginning,
We are created to touch that day
Love and Peace in Oneness with God,
Shows death is not the only way.

If a beginning has an end,
Then an end has a beginning.
Look to the Son of God,
He glorifies our beginning.

Thank God!

"OUR STEPPING STONE"

In God we pray as we stay,
But at least we open our heart;
Allowance of Christ forgives all sins,
So in death, in honor, we depart.

We depart the Earth, a world we knew,
It was only our stepping stone;
We gave to Christ what belonged to Him,
We never depart alone.

"IN EVERY SEASON"

In every season, there is reason
why we and things must die,
Understand truest sense of love,
as we laugh so must we cry.

"CLEARLY"

As we move in silence, after life,
Taking only memories and dreams,
Our empty bodies lie awaiting,
For our souls return, it seems.

We can see so much more clearly,
Our mind's eyes are opened wide,
Christ is waiting for us,
There is no reason to hide.

Our souls? soft white toward brightness,
With marked sin, only a touch,
Our belief in holy forgiveness,
We can lean on as our crutch.

"IN FULL BLOOM"

Ever, forever
And a day
We should always say
Thank You God
For we
Who live and die among the flowers
Can still live
In Afterlife
In full bloom
Rich with Son Shine
Son Shine?
Glorious Christ

"FATHER TO CHILD"

Child to Father—I don't understand?
Father to Child—Child take my hand,
Walk in glory with your Father,
For I am.

I did promise you a rainbow after the storm!

"THE SON"

J ourney after life, live in Me,
E ternally be a blessed one,
S hare with God purest of truth,
U phold The Father and The Son,
S hine in love and peace forever,

FOR I AM THE SON!

"FREEDOM"

Freedom Is:
That step from your body, to realize
Prayers have all been worth while.

"A KNOCK"

Days we've waited for our bodies to rest,
Green pastures, still waters are there;
The Lord is our shepherd we shall not want,
So gently we are lifted from fear.

We travel through the shadow of death,
Evil we will fear no more;
Afterlife is where we'll be,
Just knock, Christ opens the door.

"A BLINK AWAY"

Among these acres of love, my love,
There is an acre of peace,
It's called forever, or eternity,
A blink from life, and decease.

After life? I am as I will always be,
Purest love enhances my bloom,
I've opened my heart to The Truest Son,
For in Christ we do resume.

"TEARS OF JOY"

As you're in my thought, I'm in your thought,
We'll always be together in heart;
I've moved to the mansion in Our Father's House,
Only time will keep us apart.

Serve God with love and do your best,
Be of sharing until you depart;
Then come to the mansion in Our Father's house,
Tears of joy from you sweetheart.

"BEYOND OUR DREAMS"

I know my love you're lonely,
Please have no tears for me,
We are born but for this moment,
This pleasure—Eternity.

My body in peace is sleeping,
I have stepped to the other side,
The Afterlife, I knew was here,
Beyond my ego and pride.

Imagine purest sense of being loved,
Where hatred can't exist,
And beauty far beyond our dreams,
My days have all been kissed.

So as I move on this moment,
Please have no tears for me,
Live your life and do your best,
Together we will be.

"LIFE IS SHORT"

One day we see a rainbow,
We know our storm has passed,
The Son is shining brightly,
Eternally to last.

Dream our dreams,
Live and give,
Share with all our heart,

Life is short,
There's plenty of time,
Prepare for our new start.

Christ lives!

"HEAVEN BOUND"

We suffer in pain, again and again,
To move this world around,
Sickness, health, poverty or wealth,
Don't forget, we're heaven bound.

Heaven bound? In silence or sound,
It's forever oneness above,
Remember well this simple line,
"GOD TOUCHED US WITH HIS LOVE."

"FOR LIFE"

We live
As in the silence of a breeze
For we are
Not as we were
Our bodies rest in peace
But we move on
In love
Love is as the sun
It grows new life
New life?
Life is The Son
The Prince of Peace
The Son gives life
He gave His life
For life

"THE STORM PASSES"

Death is not as the moon
Cold
Empty of life
Death is a rainbow
As the storm passes
Death sparkles in the Son
Fear not
Christ The Son is warmth!

"REALIZE"

A sin can bring you closer to God,
REALIZE—You need ask forgiveness.

Christ always shines brightly,
REALIZE—You must also forgive
yourself.

Life is tough and there's no easy path,
REALIZE—The strength you have.

Dream and love, live and die,
REALIZE—Who died for our sins.

In one last breath there is Afterlife,
REALIZE—Prayers are always answered.

"WE ARE LOVED"

To touch the loneliness your heart must feel,
I leave my love, it will help you heal,
I'm in Afterlife, where you can't see,
But one day your soul will stand beside me.

Always we're loved by the warmth of The Son,
This is only change, in Christ we're of one,
The Prince of Peace extended His heart,
Share your love until you depart.

"A BEAM OF LIGHT"

We can step to a higher level,
Beyond ourselves and dream,
After life just lift in love,
Death is only a beam.

A beam of light that shines a sight,
We have never seen before,
Glorious Heaven above ourselves,
In equal, there is no war.

"THE TOP OF THE MOUNTAIN"

What is life but a beautiful moment,
A moment from God above,
Whether together or passing on,
Life is given with love.

God above gave us precious time,
To grow, to learn and share,
It gives a heart such joyful peace,
To know that God does care.

God does care for our eternal soul,
That is why we have free will,
Afterlife is the top of the mountain,
We've already climbed the hill.

"SENSATION"

Look above the mountains,
Beyond your dreams,
To prayer and concentration

Feel the wholeness,
Christ's shining beams,
They're a wonderful sensation.

Enhance your life with a sparkle
Christ lives!

"LITTLE LOST CHILD"

Little lost child—you are loved,
Come, we'll show you the way,
There's peace forever Afterlife,
Your parents will be here one day.

You were only to stay for a little while,
To share your love with all,
Now is your time to be with God,
For in the wind He echoed His call.

Place trust in God and open your heart,
There's no more sadness or ill,
There's only eternity filling the air,
An eternity of love is God's will.

"STARTING OVER"

This day I see more clearly,
In death my storm has passed,
The Son is shining brightly,
Eternally to last.

I dream my dreams, I live and give,
I share with all my heart,
Prepare for life, after life,
In Christ is our new start.

A promise is forever!

"CLOUDS DO PASS"

Once upon the sunshine,
Then a rainy day,
One by one the clouds do pass,
Again, a sunny day.

So, once upon the sunshine,
Then a rainy day,
One by one the clouds do pass,
Then a God's Son day.

"NOT ENOUGH KNOWING"

Part way through
Life
Not enough knowing
For God
For Christ and oneness
We keep on growing.

Part way through
Death
Not enough knowing
For God
For Christ and oneness
We keep on going.

"ASHES TO ASHES"

Lay your body in peace, the spirit moves on,
ENERGY—From The Son,
Ashes to ashes, dust to dust, be touched,
By The Holy One.

The Holy One? Christ is our Glory,
IMAGINE—Forever in His Peace,
A body may pain, a body may die,
But the soul does not know of decease.

Decease? The end, to start our beginning,
ONENESS—Forever on,
Share your life and all your goodness,
There is no such thing as gone.

"IN LOVING CARE"

As the years flow past, we're allowed some tears,
They're needed for sorrow and pain;
Tears help us grow, understand and know,
That life is of sunshine and rain.

Along life's path, be of strength and peace,
Fear not for there is no end;
In The Son there's warmth to dry any tears,
The Son is The Prince, is our Friend.

The Prince of Peace extends His Hand,
With love to build us anew;
As we grow and share in His loving care,
My friend, His prayers are with you.

"GOD'S GOLDEN RAYS"

Follow the steps of The Chosen One,
Please understand, it's all in Son,

Christ is the way to learn—achieve,
From only that moment when we believe,

Travel through forever in eternal dreams,
On God's golden rays of life's lovely beams.

"LOST LAMB"

Stillness, soft release, as I decease,
Love penetrates me,
I've grown from need, among some weed,
Into a beautiful free.

As different I am, I am no different,
The me you know, I am,
Pure perfection, perfect reflection,
Understanding little lost lamb.

Little lost lamb, I was I am,
I leave my body to cease,
With life forever after life,
I grow with God and peace.

"UNDERSTANDING"

We take a journey to freedom,
Where there is no pain or hate,
We've carried a cross throughout life,
To touch an open gate.

We see our friends from long ago,
Their smiles enhanced with love,
Warmth from The Son is filling the air,
It's pure as a virgin dove.

In life we touch others' hearts,
In caring and sharing ways,
The essence of understanding oneness,
For all eternal days.

Have no fear if death is near,
For we have an eternal Friend,
Our Brother suffered on the cross,
In Him there is no end.

"WHAT OF A ROSE"

As a rose does open on a golden day,
So it must wither and flow away,
Where is that rose that we could see?
In the glory of Heaven growing free.

"IN LIFE'S BALANCE"

One is born
And
One he dies
As
One he laughs
And
One he cries.

Too many tears
And fears of death
One is born again
In Christ!

"CHILD OF PEACE"

Child of peace, when there are tears,
They'll pass with time and love,
Feel Christ's ray, shine through your day,
Send your prayers to God above.

God above is endless love,
For Him we live and grow,
His love is like a bouquet of flowers,
With seeds to reap and sow.

"CRYSTAL AND RAINBOWS"

Go beyond your dreams, reach out and touch
Another's life, it will mean so much;
Add Crystal and Rainbows, be oh so clever
To share your beauty forever and ever.

Add life to life, be very headstrong,
Be wisdom and kindness, you'll never be wrong;
Share love and leadership, peace be your will,
May your cup overflow till your body lies still.

Then take with you the all that you know,
Spread love and sunshine, these seeds you must sow;
Plant them with honesty and everyday caring,
In life and death, we must always be sharing.

"OURSELVES"

Everything we are is because of God
Everything we are not, is because of ourselves
"May you have inner peace"

11/5/88

Sincerely,
Al Caputo

Personal Notes